SECRETS TO CULTIVATE a RESILIENT MINDSET

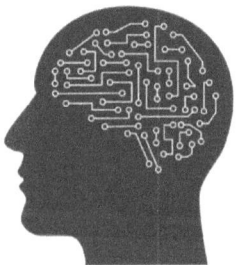

Foster a Positive Mindset, Conquer Challenges with Optimism, Master Daily Habits for Positivity, and Embrace Lasting Motivation

by

MAHUYA GUPTA

Copyright © 2024 by Mahuya Gupta

All rights reserved. No part of this book may be reproduced in any form without permission in writing from the author.

No part of this publication may be reproduced or transmitted in any form or by any means, mechanical or electronic, including photocopying or recording, by any information storage and retrieval system, or by email or any other means whatsoever without permission in writing from the author.

Table Of Contents

Introduction 5

   1. The Influence of Mindset 5

   2. Defining Positive Thinking 6

The Impact of Positive Thinking 9

   1. Psychological Benefits 9

   2. Physical Health Benefits 15

Cultivating a Positive Mindset 21

   1. Awareness of Negative Thoughts 22

   2. Reframing Negative Thoughts 26

Strategies for Positivity 37

   1. Gratitude Practices 38

   2. Affirmations and Visualization 44

Overcoming Challenges with Optimism 53

   1. Resilience in the Face of Adversity 54

   2. Positive Communication 60

Motivation and Goal Achievement 67

   1. Positive Thinking and Goal Setting 68

   2. Maintaining Motivation Throughout the Journey 72

3. Creating a Positive Work Environment 74

Daily Habits for Positivity 81

    1. Morning Rituals 81

    2. Mindfulness and Meditation 84

Conclusion 89

References 97

About the Author 101

Disclaimer 103

May I Ask You For A Small Favor? 105

Other Books Written By The Author 107

Introduction

Hello there, dear reader! Welcome to a journey that's as practical as it is transformative. Before we dive into the chapters ahead, let's have a friendly chat about something profoundly powerful—your mindset. You might have heard people say, "It's all in your mind," and wondered how true that is. Well, today, we're going to explore just how much our thoughts shape our world and determine our success.

1. The Influence of Mindset

You know, there's a fascinating connection between how we think and the way our lives unfold. Think about those days when you wake up feeling upbeat—everything seems easier, right? Conversations flow, tasks get ticked off effortlessly, and even the smallest joys shine brightly. On the flip side, we've all experienced mornings where just getting out of bed feels like a monumental task, and the day seems to drag on. The difference? It's all about our mindset.

When we talk about mindset, we're referring to the lens through which we view the world. A positive mindset isn't just about wearing a smile; it's a powerful tool that can lead to extraordinary achievements and a fulfilling life. Research shows that those who cultivate a positive outlook tend to be more resilient, more successful, and generally happier. Isn't that amazing?

This book is going to show you how embracing positivity can transform your life in ways you might not have thought possible. We'll explore the science behind positive thinking and how shifting your mindset can unlock doors to new opportunities and successes.

2. Defining Positive Thinking

So, what exactly is positive thinking? Let's break it down together. Positive thinking is about focusing on the good in any given situation and expecting favorable outcomes. It doesn't mean ignoring life's challenges or pretending everything is perfect. Instead, it's about maintaining a hopeful and optimistic outlook, even when things aren't going as planned.

Imagine a day filled with unexpected hurdles—a traffic jam, a tough meeting, or a missed deadline. A positive thinker acknowledges these setbacks but doesn't let them overshadow their day. They might say, "Alright, this is a challenge, but I can handle it." They look for solutions, learn from the experience, and move forward with a resilient spirit.

On the other hand, a negative mindset tends to dwell on problems and magnify difficulties. It's like viewing the world through a cloudy lens where every obstacle seems insurmountable. This kind of thinking can hold us back from seeing possibilities and achieving our full potential.

In the pages that follow, we'll dive deeper into what positive thinking is, how it works, and most importantly, how you can cultivate it in your own life. By understanding and harnessing the power of a positive mindset, you'll find yourself better equipped to handle life's ups and downs with grace and determination.

As we embark on this exploration together, think of me as a friend guiding you through practical steps, inspiring stories, and insightful science that will help you tap into the incredible power of positive thinking. Whether you're seeking to overcome challenges, achieve your goals, or simply live a happier life, this book will provide you with the tools and inspiration you need. Let's start this journey towards a brighter, more optimistic future together.

Warm regards,

CHAPTER 1

THE IMPACT OF POSITIVE THINKING

"Change your thoughts and you change your world."

- Norman Vincent Peale

Hello, dear friend! Welcome to our first deep dive into the incredible world of positive thinking. I'm excited to have you here as we explore how a shift in perspective can make a world of difference. Today, let's talk about the profound impacts of positive thinking on our lives. We'll start by looking at the psychological benefits and then move on to how it affects our physical health.

1. Psychological Benefits

Exploring the Positive Effects on Mental Health

Have you ever noticed how some people seem to handle life's bumps with remarkable ease? They smile through setbacks, maintain a cheerful demeanour, and bounce back quickly from disappointments. What's their secret? Often, it's their mindset. Positive thinking is a powerful tool that can significantly enhance our mental well-being.

Building Resilience and Coping Skills

Let's start with resilience. Resilience is like a mental muscle that helps us cope with challenges and bounce back from adversity. When we cultivate a positive outlook, we strengthen this muscle. Research has shown that individuals with a positive mindset are better equipped to handle stress and recover from trauma. They don't see setbacks as insurmountable problems but as opportunities for growth.

Think about a time when you faced a difficult situation. Maybe it was a job loss, a relationship breakup, or a health scare. How did you react? Did you find a way to stay hopeful and look for solutions, or did you feel overwhelmed and defeated?

Those who approach such situations with positivity often find that they're able to adapt more quickly and emerge stronger.

Reducing Anxiety and Depression

Positive thinking also plays a crucial role in reducing anxiety and depression. When we focus on the positive aspects of our lives and practice gratitude, we shift our attention away from worries and negative thoughts. This shift can help reduce the symptoms of anxiety and depression.

Cognitive-behavioural therapy (CBT), a popular and effective treatment for anxiety and depression, often incorporates elements of positive thinking. It encourages individuals to challenge their negative thoughts and replace them with more balanced, positive ones. By rethinking our automatic responses, we can break the cycle of negativity and build a healthier, more optimistic mindset.

Enhancing Emotional Well-Being

Positive thinking isn't just about being happy all the time. It's about developing a deeper sense of contentment and emotional balance. When we cultivate positive thoughts, we create a buffer against the stresses of daily life. This doesn't mean we won't experience negative emotions; it means we're better prepared to handle them.

For example, studies have shown that people who regularly practice positive thinking experience higher levels of satisfaction and lower levels of distress. They are more likely to experience positive emotions such as joy, love, and enthusiasm. These emotions, in turn, contribute to a more fulfilling and enjoyable life.

The Role of Positive Self-Talk

One of the most effective ways to foster positive thinking is through positive self-talk. This means the internal dialogue we have with ourselves. When we engage in positive self-talk, we encourage and uplift ourselves, which boosts our confidence and helps us stay motivated.

Think of it like being your own best friend. Instead of criticizing yourself for every mistake, you offer words of encouragement and support. This can be particularly helpful during challenging times, as it helps maintain our sense of self-worth and keeps us focused on finding solutions rather than dwelling on problems.

Stress Reduction and Emotional Well-Being

We live in a fast-paced world where stress is almost unavoidable. But how we handle that stress can make all the difference. Positive thinking can significantly reduce stress levels and improve our overall emotional well-being.

Perception and Stress Response

Our perception of stress plays a key role in how we experience it. When we view stressful situations with a positive outlook, we're more likely to see them as challenges rather than threats. This shift in perception can reduce the intensity of our stress response.

For instance, if you view a tight deadline at work as an opportunity to showcase your skills rather than a looming catastrophe, you're likely to approach it with more energy and less anxiety. This positive mindset helps to keep our stress hormones in check and prevents them from wreaking havoc on our bodies and minds.

Emotional Regulation

Positive thinking also enhances our ability to regulate our emotions. It helps us maintain a calm and composed demeanour, even in the face of adversity. When we train our minds to focus on the positive, we're better able to manage our emotional reactions and avoid being overwhelmed by negative feelings.

For example, consider the simple act of reframing negative thoughts. Instead of thinking, "I'm terrible at this and will never succeed," we can reframe it to, "I'm learning and improving with each attempt." This subtle shift in perspective can significantly reduce our emotional distress and help us stay focused and motivated.

Creating a Positive Feedback Loop

When we adopt a positive mindset, we create a positive feedback loop that enhances our emotional well-being. Positive thoughts lead to positive emotions, which in turn lead to positive actions. These actions reinforce our positive thoughts, creating a cycle of positivity that permeates all aspects of our lives.

For example, someone who starts their day with a positive affirmation or gratitude practice is more likely to experience positive emotions throughout the day. These emotions influence their interactions and behaviours, leading to positive outcomes that further reinforce their initial positive thoughts.

2. Physical Health Benefits

Connection Between Positive Thinking and Physical Health

We often talk about the mind-body connection, but did you know that positive thinking can have a profound impact on your physical health? Our thoughts and emotions are closely linked to our physical well-being, and cultivating a positive mindset can lead to numerous health benefits.

Boosting the Immune System

One of the most remarkable benefits of positive thinking is its ability to boost the immune system. Studies have shown that individuals who maintain a positive outlook are less susceptible to illnesses and recover more quickly when they do get sick.

The reason behind this is quite fascinating. Positive emotions and thoughts can trigger the release of beneficial hormones and neurotransmitters in our bodies. These chemicals enhance the functioning of our immune system, making it more effective at fighting off infections and diseases.

For example, a study conducted at the University of Kentucky found that optimistic individuals had a stronger immune response compared to their pessimistic counterparts. This means that a positive mindset not only makes us feel better mentally but also strengthens our body's natural defences.

Promoting Heart Health

Positive thinking is also good for your heart—literally! Research has shown that a positive mindset is associated with better cardiovascular health and a lower risk of heart disease.

One study from Harvard University found that people with a positive outlook were more likely to have healthier hearts. They had lower blood pressure, reduced levels of stress hormones, and better overall heart function. These benefits are thought to stem from the fact that positive thinkers are more likely to engage in heart-healthy behaviors such as regular exercise, healthy eating, and stress management.

Enhancing Longevity

Did you know that positive thinking could actually help you live longer? Several studies have found a correlation between a positive mindset and increased lifespan.

For instance, research from Yale University showed that individuals with a positive attitude towards aging lived, on average, 7.5 years longer than those with a more negative outlook. This remarkable finding suggests that how we think about our lives and our future can significantly influence our longevity.

Positive thinkers tend to take better care of themselves, maintain healthier relationships, and engage in activities that promote well-being. These behaviours contribute to a longer, healthier life.

Reducing the Risk of Chronic Diseases

Chronic diseases like diabetes, hypertension, and arthritis can be influenced by our mindset. Positive thinking can play a role in preventing these conditions and managing their symptoms.

For example, people with a positive outlook are more likely to adhere to medical advice, follow treatment plans, and make lifestyle changes that reduce their risk of chronic diseases. They are also better equipped to cope with the challenges posed by these conditions, leading to improved quality of life and better health outcomes.

Improving Pain Management

Pain is a complex experience that is influenced by both physical and psychological factors. Positive thinking can help manage pain more effectively by altering our perception of it.

Studies have shown that individuals who practice positive thinking techniques, such as visualization and affirmations, experience less pain and require less pain medication compared to those with a more negative outlook. This is because positive thinking can activate the brain's natural pain-relief mechanisms, making us more resilient to discomfort.

Enhancing Overall Well-Being

Positive thinking contributes to a general sense of well-being. It helps us feel more energetic, sleep better, and experience less fatigue. When we maintain a positive outlook, our bodies respond with increased vitality and a greater capacity for physical activity.

For example, positive thinkers are more likely to engage in regular exercise, which in turn boosts their mood and physical health. They are also more likely to prioritize healthy eating and adequate sleep, which are essential for overall well-being.

In wrapping up this chapter, it's clear that positive thinking isn't just a "nice to have" but a cornerstone of a healthy and fulfilling life. From bolstering our mental health to enhancing our physical well-being, a positive mindset can transform every aspect of our lives. As we move forward in this book, we'll explore practical ways to cultivate and maintain this powerful mindset, enabling us to navigate life's challenges with grace and resilience.

So, as we prepare to journey into the next chapter, I encourage you to start noticing your thoughts. Are they lifting you up or holding you back? Remember, every positive thought is a step towards a happier, healthier, and more successful life.

Chapter 2

Cultivating a Positive Mindset

"The mind is everything. What you think you become."

- Buddha

Hello again, dear friend! Welcome back. In the last chapter, we talked about the incredible impact that positive thinking can have on our mental and physical health. Today, we're going to take it a step further and discuss how to cultivate a positive mindset.

Cultivating a positive mindset isn't about ignoring the challenges or pretending everything is perfect. It's about training our minds to focus on the positive aspects of our experiences and to view difficulties as opportunities for growth.

This chapter will guide you through recognizing and understanding negative thoughts, and then, importantly, how to reframe those thoughts into positive ones.

1. Awareness of Negative Thoughts

Recognizing and Understanding Negative Thought Patterns

Let's start with the basics. Our thoughts are like the soundtrack to our daily lives. They play constantly in the background, influencing how we feel and how we act. However, not all of these thoughts are helpful. Some can be quite negative, and if left unchecked, they can shape our mindset in a way that limits our potential and well-being.

The first step in cultivating a positive mindset is becoming aware of these negative thought patterns. It's like catching yourself in the act of thinking negatively and then understanding why you're doing it. This awareness is crucial because you can't change what you don't recognize.

Common Negative Thought Patterns

Negative thought patterns can take many forms, but here are a few common ones that most of us experience from time to time:

1. **Catastrophizing**: This is when we expect the worst possible outcome in any situation. For example, if you make a mistake at work, you might immediately think, "I'm going to get fired."

2. **Overgeneralizing**: This involves seeing a single negative event as a never-ending pattern of defeat. If you have a bad day, you might think, "Nothing ever goes right for me."

3. **All-or-Nothing Thinking**: This is when we see things in black and white terms, without any middle ground. For instance, "If I'm not a complete success, I'm a total failure."

4. **Mental Filtering**: This is when we focus solely on the negatives and ignore any positives. You might have received five compliments and one criticism, but only remember the criticism.

5. **Personalizing**: This is when we blame ourselves for events outside our control. If a friend is upset, you might think, "It's my fault they're feeling this way."

Identifying Triggers for Negativity

Understanding your triggers is another essential step in managing negative thoughts. Triggers are specific situations, people, or environments that tend to provoke negative thinking. Identifying these can help you prepare and respond more effectively when they occur.

Here are some ways to pinpoint your triggers:

1. **Reflect on Your Day**: Spend a few minutes each evening thinking about your day. Were there moments when you felt particularly negative or stressed? What was happening at that time?

2. **Keep a Thought Diary**: Writing down your thoughts can be a powerful way to spot patterns. Whenever you notice yourself thinking negatively, jot down what triggered it and how you responded.

3. **Ask for Feedback**: Sometimes, those close to us can see our triggers more clearly than we can. Ask a trusted friend or family member if they've noticed

situations that seem to bring out negative thoughts in you.

4. **Observe Physical Responses**: Our bodies often react to triggers before we're even aware of them. Pay attention to signs like increased heart rate, muscle tension, or feeling hot. These can be clues that something is triggering a negative response.

Understanding the Origins of Negative Thoughts

Once you've identified your triggers, it's helpful to understand where these negative thoughts are coming from. Often, they are rooted in past experiences or deeply held beliefs about ourselves and the world.

For example, if you grew up in an environment where you were frequently criticized, you might have developed a habit of expecting the worst or doubting your abilities.

Recognizing these roots can help you understand why certain triggers affect you and start to challenge those ingrained beliefs.

2. Reframing Negative Thoughts

Strategies for Transforming Negative Thoughts into Positive Ones

Now that we've talked about recognizing and understanding negative thoughts, let's move on to how we can transform them. Reframing is a powerful technique that involves changing the way we interpret situations and our reactions to them. It's about looking at things from a different perspective and finding the positive in the negative.

Practice Gratitude

One of the simplest and most effective ways to reframe negative thoughts is to practice gratitude. When we focus on what we're thankful for, it shifts our attention away from what's wrong and towards what's right.

Start by setting aside a few minutes each day to think about or write down things you're grateful for. They don't have to be big things—small blessings count too. Maybe it's the warmth of the sun on your face, a kind word from a friend, or the fact that you made it through a challenging day. Over time, this practice can help rewire your brain to focus more on the positives in your life.

Challenge Negative Thoughts

Another effective strategy is to challenge your negative thoughts directly. When you notice a negative thought, ask yourself questions to test its validity. This process is often called cognitive restructuring.

For example, if you catch yourself thinking, "I always mess things up," ask yourself, "Is that true? Can I think of times when I succeeded?" This helps you break the habit of overgeneralizing and replace it with a more balanced perspective.

Use Positive Affirmations

Positive affirmations are statements that reinforce positive beliefs about yourself and your abilities. They can be a powerful tool for counteracting negative self-talk.

Create a list of affirmations that resonate with you, such as "I am capable," "I deserve happiness," or "I can handle whatever comes my way." Repeat these affirmations to yourself regularly, especially when you're feeling down or doubting yourself. Over time, they can help build your confidence and shift your mindset towards positivity.

Visualize Positive Outcomes

Visualization is another technique that can help you reframe negative thoughts. Instead of focusing on what could go wrong, take a moment to imagine a positive outcome. Picture yourself succeeding, feeling happy, or overcoming a challenge.

For example, if you're nervous about an upcoming presentation, visualize yourself speaking confidently and receiving positive feedback from your audience. This can help reduce anxiety and boost your confidence.

Cognitive Restructuring Techniques

Cognitive restructuring is a therapeutic technique that involves changing the way we think about challenging situations. It's a structured approach to reframing negative thoughts and can be incredibly effective in cultivating a positive mindset.

Here's a step-by-step guide to cognitive restructuring:

1. **Identify the Negative Thought**: Start by recognizing the negative thought. What exactly are you thinking, and what triggered it?

2. **Examine the Evidence**: Next, look at the evidence for and against this thought. Is it based on facts, or is it an assumption? Are there alternative explanations?

3. **Consider Alternative Perspectives**: Think about how someone else might view the situation. What would you say to a friend who was thinking the same way? This can help you see things from a different angle.

4. **Challenge the Thought**: Ask yourself questions to challenge the negative thought. For example, "What's the worst that could happen, and how likely is it?" or "What are some other ways to look at this situation?"

5. **Replace with a Positive Thought**: Finally, replace the negative thought with a more positive or balanced one. This doesn't mean denying reality but finding a constructive way to think about it.

Example of Cognitive Restructuring

Let's say you're feeling anxious about a job interview and thinking, "I'm going to mess up and not get the job."

1. **Identify the Thought**: "I'm going to mess up and not get the job."

2. **Examine the Evidence**: What evidence do you have that you will mess up? Have you succeeded in similar situations before? Is it possible that you could perform well?

3. **Consider Alternative Perspectives**: How would a friend view this situation? They might say, "You've prepared well, and you have the skills they're looking for."

4. **Challenge the Thought**: What's the worst that could happen if you don't get the job? Can you handle it? What are the chances that you will actually mess up?

5. **Replace with a Positive Thought**: "I've prepared well, and I have the skills they need. I'll do my best, and that's enough."

Mindfulness and Thought Awareness

Mindfulness is another valuable tool for cultivating a positive mindset. It involves being fully present in the moment and observing your thoughts without judgment. This awareness allows you to notice negative thoughts as they arise and choose how to respond to them.

By practicing mindfulness, you can learn to catch negative thoughts early and reframe them before they spiral into a full-blown negative mindset. This practice can also help you develop a more compassionate attitude towards yourself, reducing the tendency to be overly critical or harsh.

How to Practice Mindfulness

1. **Set Aside Time:** Find a few minutes each day to practice mindfulness. This can be done through meditation or simply by sitting quietly and focusing on your breath.

2. **Observe Your Thoughts:** As you sit quietly, observe your thoughts as they come and go. Try not to get caught up in them or judge them. Just notice them.

3. **Return to the Present Moment:** Whenever you find yourself getting lost in thoughts, gently bring your attention back to your breath or the sensations in your body.

4. **Practice Non-Judgment:** Practice observing your thoughts without labeling them as good or bad. This can help you develop a more accepting and balanced view of your thoughts and emotions.

Developing a Growth Mindset

A growth mindset is the belief that our abilities and intelligence can be developed through effort and learning. This contrasts with a fixed mindset, which holds that our abilities are static and unchangeable.

Cultivating a growth mindset is closely linked to positive thinking because it encourages us to see challenges as opportunities to grow rather than as threats. When we adopt a growth mindset, we're more likely to embrace learning and persist in the face of difficulties.

How to Foster a Growth Mindset

1. **Embrace Challenges**: Instead of avoiding difficult tasks, view them as opportunities to learn and grow. Remind yourself that every challenge is a chance to improve.

2. **Learn from Criticism**: Rather than taking criticism personally, see it as valuable feedback that can help you improve. Ask yourself, "What can I learn from this?"

3. **Celebrate Effort**: Focus on the effort you put into tasks rather than just the outcome. Recognize that persistence and hard work are valuable, regardless of the immediate results.

4. **Keep Learning**: Stay curious and open to new experiences. Whether it's a new skill, a different perspective, or a challenging situation, see each one as a chance to grow.

In conclusion, cultivating a positive mindset is about more than just thinking happy thoughts. It involves recognizing and understanding our negative thought patterns, identifying our triggers, and actively working to reframe those thoughts in a more positive light.

By practicing gratitude, challenging negative thoughts, using positive affirmations, and fostering a growth mindset, we can train our minds to focus on the positive and transform our lives.

As you move forward, remember that this is a journey. Be patient with yourself and celebrate each step you take towards a more positive mindset. Your thoughts have the power to shape your world, so let's start shaping a world filled with optimism, resilience, and joy.

Chapter 3

Strategies for Positivity

"Gratitude unlocks the fullness of life. It turns what we have into enough, and more. It turns denial into acceptance, chaos to order, confusion to clarity."

*- **Melody Beattie***

Hello again, my friend! We've talked about the impacts of positive thinking and how to cultivate a positive mindset. Now, let's explore some practical strategies that can help you bring more positivity into your daily life.

Today, we'll dive into two powerful practices: gratitude and affirmations. These are not just feel-good techniques; they are grounded in science and have profound effects on our mental and emotional well-being.

So, let's explore how these simple yet profound tools can help you build a more positive, fulfilling life.

1. Gratitude Practices

Keeping a Gratitude Journal

One of the most effective ways to cultivate positivity is through the practice of gratitude. When we take the time to acknowledge and appreciate the good things in our lives, we shift our focus away from what we lack and towards what we have. This simple shift in perspective can have a profound impact on our overall outlook.

A wonderful way to practice gratitude is by keeping a gratitude journal. This is a personal space where you can record the things you're thankful for each day. The act of writing down your blessings helps to solidify them in your mind and creates a tangible record of the positive aspects of your life.

How to Start a Gratitude Journal

Starting a gratitude journal is easy and can be done with just a few minutes each day. Here are some tips to get you started:

1. **Choose Your Journal**: Find a notebook or journal that you enjoy writing in. It could be a fancy leather-bound book, a simple spiral notebook, or even a digital app on your phone or computer.

2. **Set a Regular Time**: Choose a time of day that works best for you to reflect on your gratitude. Many people find that writing in their journal before bed helps them end the day on a positive note. Others prefer to do it first thing in the morning to set a positive tone for the day.

3. **Write Down 3-5 Things Each Day**: Start by writing down three to five things you're grateful for each day. They can be big or small, specific or general. The important thing is to focus on what made you feel good or what you appreciate.

4. **Be Specific**: Try to be as specific as possible. Instead of writing "I'm grateful for my family," you might write "I'm grateful for the hug my daughter gave me today." Specific details make the practice more meaningful and help you recall positive experiences more vividly.

5. **Reflect on the Positive Emotions**: As you write, take a moment to reflect on the positive emotions associated with each item. Relive the joy, peace, or contentment you felt. This deepens the impact of the gratitude practice.

Benefits of a Gratitude Journal

Keeping a gratitude journal offers numerous benefits:

1. **Increased Happiness**: Regularly reflecting on what you're grateful for can boost your overall happiness. It helps you focus on the positive aspects of your life and fosters a sense of contentment.

2. **Improved Emotional Resilience**: Gratitude helps build emotional resilience. When you make it a habit to focus on the positives, you're better equipped to handle life's challenges and setbacks.

3. **Better Relationships**: Expressing gratitude can improve your relationships. When you acknowledge and appreciate the good in others, it strengthens your connections and fosters positive interactions.

4. **Reduced Stress**: Focusing on what you're thankful for can help reduce stress and anxiety. It shifts your attention away from worries and towards what's good in your life.

5. **Enhanced Well-Being**: Overall, gratitude contributes to a greater sense of well-being. It promotes a positive mindset and encourages you to see the good in everyday life.

Recognizing and Appreciating the Positive Aspects of Life

Gratitude goes beyond keeping a journal; it's about developing a mindset that consistently recognizes and appreciates the positive aspects of life. This can be particularly challenging when we're going through tough times, but it's often when we need gratitude the most.

Practicing Mindful Appreciation

Mindful appreciation is about being present and fully experiencing the good moments in our lives. It's taking the time to savor positive experiences and truly acknowledge them. Here's how you can incorporate mindful appreciation into your daily routine:

1. **Pause and Notice:** Throughout your day, make a conscious effort to pause and notice the good things happening around you. It could be a beautiful sunrise, a warm cup of coffee, or a kind gesture from a colleague.

2. **Savor the Moment:** When you notice something positive, take a moment to savor it. Fully immerse yourself in the experience and let it fill you with a sense of gratitude.

3. **Express Appreciation:** Whenever possible, express your appreciation to others. If someone does something kind for you, take a moment to thank them and acknowledge their gesture. This not only reinforces your gratitude but also strengthens your relationships.

4. **Reflect on Your Day:** At the end of each day, take a few minutes to reflect on the positive experiences you had. Think about what made you smile, laugh, or

feel good. This practice can help you end your day on a positive note and reinforce your sense of gratitude.

Gratitude in Challenging Times

It's easy to feel grateful when things are going well, but how do we practice gratitude during challenging times? Here are some tips for maintaining a grateful mindset even when life is tough:

1. **Focus on What You Can Control**: When facing difficulties, try to focus on what you can control rather than what you can't. Look for small things to be grateful for, even in the midst of challenges.

2. **Find Silver Linings**: Look for the silver linings in difficult situations. Ask yourself, "What can I learn from this?" or "How can this experience make me stronger?" Finding meaning in adversity can help you stay positive.

3. **Lean on Your Support System**: During tough times, lean on your support system and express gratitude for the people who are there for you.

Acknowledge their support and let them know how much you appreciate them.

4. **Practice Self-Compassion:** Be kind to yourself during challenging times. Recognize that it's okay to feel down and that you're doing your best. Practicing self-compassion can help you maintain a positive outlook.

2. Affirmations and Visualization

Creating and Using Positive Affirmations

Affirmations are positive statements that you repeat to yourself to challenge and overcome negative thoughts. They can be powerful tools for building self-confidence, motivation, and a positive mindset. By regularly affirming positive beliefs, you can reprogram your mind to focus on your strengths and capabilities.

How to Create Effective Affirmations

Creating effective affirmations is about finding statements that resonate with you and reflect the positive qualities or goals you want to cultivate. Here are some tips for creating your own affirmations:

1. **Be Specific and Personal**: Make your affirmations specific to you and your goals. Instead of a general statement like "I am successful," you might say, "I am capable of achieving my career goals."

2. **Use Positive Language**: Frame your affirmations in positive terms. Focus on what you want to achieve or feel, rather than what you want to avoid. For example, say "I am confident and capable" instead of "I don't feel insecure."

3. **Keep Them Present Tense**: Write your affirmations in the present tense as if they are already true. This helps you internalize them and feel their positive impact immediately. For example, say "I am calm and centered" instead of "I will be calm and centered."

4. **Make Them Believable**: Choose affirmations that feel believable and realistic to you. They should stretch you a little but still be within reach. If an affirmation feels too far-fetched, it might not be as effective.

5. **Keep Them Short and Simple**: Short and simple affirmations are easier to remember and repeat. Focus on a few key statements that resonate with you rather than creating a long list.

How to Use Affirmations Effectively

Once you've created your affirmations, it's important to use them regularly to reinforce their positive impact. Here's how you can incorporate affirmations into your daily routine:

1. **Repeat Them Daily**: Set aside a few minutes each day to repeat your affirmations. This could be in the morning to start your day with positivity, or in the evening as a way to wind down.

2. **Say Them Aloud**: Saying your affirmations out loud can make them more powerful. Hearing your own voice reinforces the positive message and helps you internalize it more deeply.

3. **Write Them Down**: Writing your affirmations in a journal or on sticky notes that you place around

your home or workspace can serve as visual reminders. Seeing them regularly reinforces their message.

4. **Pair Them with Visualization**: Combine your affirmations with visualization to make them even more effective. As you repeat your affirmations, close your eyes and imagine yourself experiencing the positive outcomes they describe.

5. **Believe in Them**: Believe in the power of your affirmations. Trust that they are helping you build a positive mindset and move closer to your goals.

Visualization Techniques for Goal Achievement

Visualization is a powerful technique that involves creating a mental image of your desired outcomes. By vividly imagining your goals and the steps to achieve them, you can boost your motivation, focus, and confidence.

Visualization can be particularly effective when combined with affirmations, creating a powerful synergy that propels you towards your dreams.

How to Practice Effective Visualization

Here's a step-by-step guide to practicing visualization for goal achievement:

1. **Set Clear Goals**: Start by clearly defining your goals. What do you want to achieve? Be as specific as possible. Instead of a vague goal like "I want to be successful," define what success looks like to you.

2. **Create a Detailed Mental Image**: Close your eyes and create a detailed mental image of achieving your goal. Imagine every aspect of the experience—the sights, sounds, and feelings associated with reaching your goal. The more vivid and detailed your visualization, the more powerful it will be.

3. **Engage All Your Senses**: Engage all your senses in your visualization. If your goal is to run a marathon, imagine the sound of your feet hitting the pavement, the sight of the finish line, the cheers from the crowd, and the feeling of crossing the line.

4. **Focus on the Positive Emotions**: Focus on the positive emotions you'll feel when you achieve your

goal. Feel the joy, pride, and excitement. These emotions help reinforce your motivation and commitment to your goal.

5. **Practice Regularly**: Make visualization a regular part of your routine. Spend a few minutes each day visualizing your goals and the steps to achieve them. The more you practice, the more ingrained these positive images will become in your mind.

6. **Combine with Affirmations**: Combine your visualization with affirmations to enhance its impact. As you visualize your goals, repeat your affirmations to reinforce the positive beliefs and attitudes that will help you achieve them.

Benefits of Visualization

Visualization offers numerous benefits for goal achievement and personal growth:

1. **Boosts Motivation**: Visualizing your goals and the rewards of achieving them can boost your motivation and drive. It helps you stay focused and committed, even when challenges arise.

2. **Increases Confidence**: Regularly visualizing success can increase your confidence and belief in your abilities. When you see yourself achieving your goals, it reinforces your self-efficacy and resilience.

3. **Enhances Performance**: Visualization can enhance performance in various areas, from sports to academics to professional achievements. It helps you mentally rehearse and prepare for success.

4. **Reduces Anxiety**: Visualizing positive outcomes can reduce anxiety and stress. It shifts your focus away from potential failures and towards the positive possibilities.

5. **Promotes a Positive Mindset**: Visualization fosters a positive mindset by reinforcing positive images and emotions. It helps you stay optimistic and solution-focused, even in the face of challenges.

In summary, incorporating gratitude practices, affirmations, and visualization into your daily routine can significantly enhance your positivity and overall well-being. These strategies help you focus on the positive aspects of your life, reinforce your strengths, and move confidently towards your goals.

As you continue your journey towards cultivating a positive mindset, remember that these practices are tools you can use to create a more fulfilling and joyful life. Keep practicing, stay patient, and celebrate the small victories along the way. The more you embrace these strategies, the more you'll see the transformative power of positivity in your life.

CHAPTER 4

OVERCOMING CHALLENGES WITH OPTIMISM

"When life throws challenge your way, it's not the end of the world. Rather, it's an opportunity to rise, to grow, and to shine even brighter."

- Sri Gaur Gopal Das

Hello again, my dear reader. It's wonderful to have you back as we journey further into the world of positivity. Today, we'll explore a topic that's essential for anyone looking to live a fulfilling life: overcoming challenges with optimism. Challenges and setbacks are a part of life. But with the right mindset, we can not only navigate these difficulties but also use them as steppingstones to greater success and fulfilment.

In this chapter, we'll delve into how we can cultivate resilience in the face of adversity and the role of positive communication in building a strong support network. These strategies are vital tools for maintaining optimism and thriving, no matter what life throws at us.

1. Resilience in the Face of Adversity

Life is full of ups and downs. Whether it's personal setbacks, professional challenges, or unexpected crises, how we respond to adversity significantly influences our well-being and success. Resilience—the ability to bounce back from difficulties—is not something we're born with; it's a skill we can develop and strengthen over time.

Developing a Resilient Mindset

Developing resilience starts with our mindset. It's about how we perceive and respond to challenges. A resilient mindset allows us to see setbacks not as insurmountable obstacles, but as opportunities for growth and learning.

Key Components of a Resilient Mindset

1. **Accepting Reality**: Resilience begins with accepting reality as it is, rather than wishing for it to be different. This doesn't mean resigning ourselves to circumstances, but acknowledging them as the starting point for action.

2. **Optimistic Outlook**: Optimism is a cornerstone of resilience. It's the belief that things can and will get better. This positive outlook motivates us to keep going, even when the going gets tough.

3. **Purpose and Meaning**: Finding purpose and meaning in adversity helps us to persevere. When we see challenges as meaningful experiences that contribute to our growth, we're more likely to stay motivated and resilient.

4. **Self-Compassion**: Being kind to ourselves during difficult times is crucial. Recognizing that setbacks are a normal part of life and treating ourselves with the same compassion we would offer a friend can bolster our resilience.

Strategies to Build Resilience

Building resilience involves cultivating these components through practical strategies. Here are some ways to develop a resilient mindset:

1. **Reframe Negative Thoughts**: When faced with a challenge, try to reframe your negative thoughts into positive or neutral ones. Instead of thinking, "I can't handle this," tell yourself, "This is tough, but I can find a way through it." This shift in perspective helps you stay focused on solutions rather than problems.

2. **Set Realistic Goals**: Break down large challenges into smaller, manageable goals. This makes it easier to take action and reduces feelings of overwhelm. Celebrate small victories along the way to maintain motivation.

3. **Develop Problem-Solving Skills**: Strengthen your problem-solving skills by regularly challenging yourself to find solutions to everyday problems. This practice builds your confidence and prepares you to handle bigger challenges more effectively.

4. **Cultivate Flexibility**: Flexibility is about being open to change and adapting to new circumstances. Practice flexibility by being willing to adjust your plans and expectations when things don't go as anticipated. This adaptability is key to resilience.

5. **Build a Support Network**: Having a strong support network is crucial for resilience. Surround yourself with people who provide emotional support, offer different perspectives, and help you stay grounded during tough times.

6. **Practice Self-Care**: Taking care of your physical and emotional well-being is vital for resilience. Regular exercise, adequate sleep, healthy eating, and activities that bring you joy and relaxation all contribute to your ability to cope with stress and bounce back from challenges.

Learning from Setbacks and Failures

Setbacks and failures are inevitable parts of life, but they don't have to define us. Instead, they can be valuable learning opportunities that help us grow and improve.

How to Learn from Setbacks

1. **Reflect on the Experience:** Take time to reflect on what happened. What went wrong? What could you have done differently? What did you learn from the experience? Reflecting on these questions helps you gain insights and avoid making the same mistakes in the future.

2. **Focus on Growth:** Instead of seeing setbacks as failures, view them as opportunities for growth. Ask yourself, "How can I grow from this experience?" This mindset shift helps you stay positive and open to learning.

3. **Seek Feedback:** Don't be afraid to seek feedback from others. Constructive feedback provides valuable perspectives and can help you improve. Be open to learning from others and incorporating their insights into your future actions.

4. **Stay Persistent:** Resilience is about persistence. When you encounter setbacks, remind yourself why you started and stay committed to your goals. Keep

going, even when progress is slow. Persistence is often the key to overcoming challenges.

5. **Celebrate Your Progress**: Acknowledge and celebrate the progress you've made, even if it's small. Recognizing your achievements boosts your confidence and motivation, making it easier to keep moving forward.

Case Study: Thomas Edison

Consider the story of Thomas Edison, the inventor of the lightbulb. Edison is famous for his persistence and resilience. He encountered countless failures and setbacks during his experiments. When asked about his failures, he famously said, "I have not failed. I've just found 10,000 ways that won't work."

Edison's ability to learn from his mistakes and keep going despite numerous setbacks ultimately led to his groundbreaking success. His story is a powerful example of how resilience and a positive mindset can help us overcome even the most daunting challenges.

2. Positive Communication

Communication plays a crucial role in how we navigate challenges and build our support networks. Positive communication fosters strong relationships, reduces conflict, and creates an environment where optimism and collaboration can thrive.

Impact of Positive Language on Personal and Professional Relationships

The words we use and the way we communicate can have a profound impact on our relationships. Positive communication involves using language that is encouraging, supportive, and constructive. It's about focusing on solutions rather than problems and building others up rather than tearing them down.

Key Elements of Positive Communication

1. **Active Listening:** Active listening is about fully engaging with the person you're communicating with. It involves listening without interrupting, asking clarifying questions, and reflecting back what you've

heard. Active listening shows respect and fosters deeper connections.

2. **Encouragement and Praise**: Offering encouragement and praise helps to build confidence and motivation in others. Be specific in your praise and acknowledge the effort and progress people are making. This positive reinforcement strengthens relationships and fosters a supportive environment.

3. **Constructive Feedback**: When providing feedback, focus on being constructive rather than critical. Highlight what the person did well and offer specific suggestions for improvement. Use "I" statements to express how their actions affected you and avoid blaming or shaming.

4. **Positive Language**: Use positive language that emphasizes solutions and possibilities. Instead of saying "We can't do this," say "What can we do to solve this problem?" This shift in language encourages a problem-solving mindset and promotes optimism.

5. **Empathy and Understanding**: Practice empathy by trying to understand the other person's perspective

and feelings. Show that you care about their experience and validate their emotions. These builds trust and deepens your connection.

Benefits of Positive Communication

Positive communication has numerous benefits for both personal and professional relationships:

1. **Strengthened Relationships:** Positive communication fosters stronger, more trusting relationships. When people feel heard, valued, and supported, they're more likely to open up and engage with you.

2. **Reduced Conflict:** Using positive language and focusing on solutions helps to reduce conflict and misunderstandings. It promotes a collaborative approach to problem-solving and minimizes negative interactions.

3. **Enhanced Teamwork:** In professional settings, positive communication enhances teamwork and collaboration. It encourages open sharing of ideas and

creates an environment where everyone feels valued and motivated to contribute.

4. **Increased Motivation**: Positive reinforcement and encouragement boost motivation and morale. When people receive positive feedback and feel appreciated, they're more likely to stay engaged and motivated.

5. **Improved Mental Health**: Positive communication contributes to better mental health and well-being. It reduces stress, fosters a sense of belonging, and creates a more supportive and positive environment.

Building a Positive and Supportive Network

Our relationships and social networks play a crucial role in how we cope with challenges and maintain a positive outlook. Building a positive and supportive network involves surrounding ourselves with people who uplift and encourage us, and who contribute to our growth and well-being.

How to Build a Positive Network

1. **Seek Out Positive Influences:** Surround yourself with people who have a positive outlook and who support your growth and well-being. Look for individuals who inspire you, encourage you, and challenge you to be your best self.

2. **Nurture Relationships:** Invest time and effort in nurturing your relationships. Be there for others, offer support and encouragement, and express your appreciation for their presence in your life. Strong relationships are built on mutual respect, trust, and care.

3. **Be a Positive Influence:** Strive to be a positive influence in others' lives. Offer encouragement, share your positivity, and be a source of support and inspiration. When you uplift others, you contribute to a positive and supportive network.

4. **Engage in Positive Activities:** Participate in activities and communities that promote positivity and personal growth. This could be joining a club, participating in volunteer work, or engaging in hobbies

that bring you joy and connect you with like-minded individuals.

5. **Set Boundaries**: Protect your well-being by setting boundaries with people who are consistently negative or draining. It's important to prioritize relationships that contribute to your positivity and well-being.

In conclusion, overcoming challenges with optimism involves cultivating resilience and practicing positive communication. By developing a resilient mindset, we can navigate setbacks and use them as opportunities for growth. Positive communication strengthens our relationships and builds a supportive network that helps us thrive.

As you continue your journey towards positivity, remember that challenges are not roadblocks but steppingstones. Embrace them with optimism, and you'll find yourself growing stronger and more resilient with each experience. And always cherish the power of positive communication—it's the key to building meaningful connections and creating a supportive environment where everyone can flourish.

Thank you for joining me in this chapter. I look forward to exploring more strategies for positivity with you in the next one. Stay positive and keep shining!

Chapter 5

Motivation and Goal Achievement

"Motivation is what gets you started. Habit is what keeps you going."

- Jim Ryun

Welcome back, dear reader. Today, let's explore how positive thinking can be your best ally on the path to achieving your goals and staying motivated. Whether you're aiming to climb the corporate ladder, start your own business, or simply live a more fulfilling life, your mindset and environment play crucial roles.

In this chapter, we'll dive into how aligning your goals with a positive mindset can sustain your motivation. We'll also look at how creating a positive work environment can foster collaboration and innovation, making your professional journey not just successful, but also joyful.

1. Positive Thinking and Goal Setting

Setting goals is the first step towards turning the invisible into the visible. However, setting goals is not enough. Aligning them with a positive mindset is what fuels your journey and keeps you motivated even when the going gets tough.

Aligning Goals with a Positive Mindset

Positive thinking doesn't mean ignoring challenges or pretending everything is perfect. It's about approaching your goals with a belief that you can achieve them, regardless of the obstacles you might face.

The Power of Positive Thinking in Goal Setting

1. **Vision and Clarity**: Positive thinking helps you to clearly define your goals. When you believe in positive outcomes, you're more likely to set ambitious yet achievable goals. You visualize not just the end result, but also the steps you need to take to get there.

2. **Optimism and Resilience**: A positive mindset fosters optimism. When you encounter setbacks,

optimism encourages you to view them as temporary obstacles rather than insurmountable barriers. This resilience keeps you moving forward, no matter how challenging the journey becomes.

3. **Increased Motivation**: Believing in your ability to achieve your goals boosts your motivation. You're more likely to put in the effort and stay committed because you trust that your hard work will pay off.

4. **Focus on Solutions**: Positive thinkers focus on finding solutions rather than dwelling on problems. This proactive approach helps you overcome obstacles and stay on track towards your goals.

Practical Tips for Aligning Goals with a Positive Mindset

1. **Set SMART Goals**: SMART goals are Specific, Measurable, Achievable, Relevant, and Time-bound. Clear and realistic goals aligned with a positive mindset provide direction and keep you focused.

   o **Specific**: Define what exactly you want to achieve.

- **Measurable:** Determine how you will measure your progress.
- **Achievable:** Set goals that are challenging yet attainable.
- **Relevant:** Ensure your goals are aligned with your values and long-term objectives.
- **Time-bound:** Set a deadline for achieving your goals.

2. **Visualize Success:** Spend time visualizing your success. Picture yourself achieving your goals and experiencing the positive emotions that come with it. This mental imagery reinforces your belief in your ability to succeed and keeps you motivated.

3. **Use Positive Affirmations:** Affirmations are positive statements that help you stay focused and motivated. Repeat affirmations that align with your goals, such as "I am capable of achieving my dreams" or "I am resilient and can overcome any challenge."

4. **Celebrate Small Wins:** Acknowledge and celebrate your progress, no matter how small.

Recognizing your achievements boosts your confidence and motivates you to keep going.

5. **Stay Flexible**: Be open to adjusting your goals as needed. Life is unpredictable, and being flexible allows you to adapt to changes and stay aligned with your positive mindset.

Case Study: Setting Goals with Positivity

Consider the story of Oprah Winfrey. Despite facing significant challenges in her early life, Oprah set ambitious goals for herself and approached them with a positive mindset. She believed in her ability to succeed and worked tirelessly towards her dreams. Her story is a powerful testament to how aligning goals with positivity can lead to extraordinary achievements.

Oprah's journey wasn't smooth, but her positive outlook and resilience kept her going. She visualized her success, stayed committed to her goals, and adapted to challenges along the way. Today, she is not only a successful media mogul but also an inspiration to millions around the world.

2. Maintaining Motivation Throughout the Journey

Motivation is the driving force that propels you towards your goals. However, maintaining motivation over the long haul can be challenging. Here's how positive thinking can help you stay motivated throughout your journey.

Strategies for Sustaining Motivation

1. **Find Your 'Why'**: Understanding why you want to achieve your goals is crucial. Your 'why' gives your goals meaning and purpose. When your motivation wanes, reconnecting with your 'why' can reignite your passion and keep you going.

2. **Break Goals into Smaller Steps**: Large goals can be overwhelming. Breaking them into smaller, manageable steps makes the journey less daunting and more achievable. Each small step you complete builds momentum and keeps you motivated.

3. **Create a Positive Environment**: Surround yourself with positivity. This includes not just positive

people, but also a physical environment that inspires and energizes you. A clutter-free, organized, and inviting space can enhance your focus and motivation.

4. **Stay Accountable**: Share your goals with someone you trust and who can hold you accountable. Regular check-ins with a mentor, friend, or coach can keep you on track and provide the support and encouragement you need.

5. **Practice Self-Care**: Taking care of your physical and emotional well-being is essential for maintaining motivation. Regular exercise, healthy eating, adequate sleep, and activities that bring you joy all contribute to sustained motivation.

6. **Stay Positive in the Face of Challenges**: Challenges and setbacks are part of the journey. Maintaining a positive mindset during tough times helps you stay motivated and focused on your goals. Remember, every obstacle is an opportunity to learn and grow.

Case Study: Marathon Training

Training for a marathon is a perfect example of the importance of maintaining motivation over a long journey. Marathon runners set a clear goal—to complete the race—and they break it down into smaller, manageable training milestones. They stay motivated by visualizing their success, celebrating small achievements, and staying accountable to their training plans. Even when the going gets tough, their positive mindset and commitment keep them moving forward.

3. Creating a Positive Work Environment

A positive work environment is not just about physical surroundings; it's about creating a culture that fosters positivity, collaboration, and innovation. Such an environment not only enhances productivity but also contributes to the overall well-being and satisfaction of everyone involved.

Fostering Positivity in the Workplace

Creating a positive work environment involves fostering a culture where positivity thrives. This means promoting open communication, mutual respect, and a sense of community.

Strategies for Fostering Positivity

1. **Encourage Open Communication**: Open and honest communication is the foundation of a positive work environment. Encourage team members to share their ideas, feedback, and concerns. This builds trust and fosters a sense of belonging.

2. **Recognize and Reward Efforts**: Acknowledge and celebrate the efforts and achievements of your team members. Recognition can be as simple as a thank-you note or as elaborate as a company-wide celebration. Regularly acknowledging contributions boosts morale and motivation.

3. **Promote Work-Life Balance**: Support your team in maintaining a healthy work-life balance. Encourage regular breaks, flexible working hours, and time off to recharge. A balanced approach to work prevents burnout and fosters long-term productivity and well-being.

4. **Create a Supportive Culture**: Cultivate a culture of support and collaboration. Encourage team members to help and support each other and create opportunities for team-building activities. A supportive culture strengthens relationships and enhances overall positivity.

5. **Foster Growth and Development**: Provide opportunities for personal and professional growth. Encourage continuous learning, offer training and development programs, and support career advancement. When people feel they are growing, they are more engaged and positive.

Encouraging Collaboration and Innovation

Collaboration and innovation thrive in a positive environment. When people feel valued and supported, they are more likely to collaborate effectively and contribute innovative ideas.

Strategies for Encouraging Collaboration and Innovation

1. **Create a Safe Space for Ideas:** Foster an environment where team members feel safe to share their ideas without fear of criticism or rejection. Encourage brainstorming sessions and open discussions where all ideas are welcomed and valued.

2. **Encourage Cross-Functional Collaboration:** Break down silos and encourage collaboration across different departments and teams. This cross-functional approach brings diverse perspectives and fosters innovation.

3. **Provide Resources and Support:** Ensure that your team has the resources and support they need to innovate. This includes providing access to the latest tools and technologies, as well as training and development opportunities.

4. **Celebrate Innovation:** Recognize and celebrate innovative ideas and initiatives. Highlight successes and learn from failures. Celebrating innovation

encourages more of it and creates a culture where creativity is valued and rewarded.

5. **Lead by Example:** As a leader, model the behavior you want to see. Demonstrate openness to new ideas, collaborate with others, and approach challenges with a positive mindset. Your behavior sets the tone for the entire team.

In conclusion, positive thinking and a supportive environment are powerful tools for achieving your goals and maintaining motivation. Aligning your goals with a positive mindset helps you stay focused and resilient, while creating a positive work environment fosters collaboration and innovation.

As you continue your journey toward achieving your goals and aspirations, remember the profound impact of maintaining a positive mindset and cultivating a supportive environment. By aligning your goals with positivity, you set the stage for success and perseverance, even in the face of challenges. Maintaining motivation requires not just setting goals, but also nurturing them with a steadfast belief in your ability to overcome obstacles and achieve greatness.

Additionally, creating a positive work environment isn't merely about enhancing productivity—it's about fostering a culture where individuals thrive, collaborate effectively, and innovate freely. When positivity permeates your workplace, it becomes a catalyst for creativity, teamwork, and overall satisfaction among your team members.

As you reflect on the insights shared in this chapter, consider how you can apply these principles in your own journey toward goal achievement. Whether in your personal pursuits or professional endeavours, let positivity guide your actions, inspire your interactions, and propel you towards a future filled with fulfilment and success.

In the next chapter, we will explore daily habits that support a positive mindset and empower you to sustain your journey of growth and achievement. Until then, stay motivated, stay positive, and continue striving for the greatness that awaits you.

Thank you for joining me on this exploration of motivation and goal achievement. Together, we can create a brighter and more fulfilling future, one positive step at a time.

Chapter 6

Daily Habits for Positivity

"It is in your moments of decision that your destiny is shaped."

- Tony Robbins

Welcome, dear reader, to the final chapter of our journey together—a chapter dedicated to exploring daily habits that cultivate positivity and nurture a resilient mindset. In our fast-paced lives, where every moment counts, these simple yet profound habits can make a significant difference in how we experience each day and how we approach life's challenges with optimism.

1. Morning Rituals

Morning rituals set the tone for your entire day. They provide an opportunity to intentionally shape your mindset and emotional state, influencing how you navigate through the hours ahead. Let's explore how you can establish a positive morning routine that energizes you and prepares you to face the day with positivity.

Establishing a Positive Morning Routine

1. **Start with Gratitude:** Begin your day by expressing gratitude for the blessings in your life. This simple practice shifts your focus from what might be lacking to what you already have, fostering a sense of abundance and positivity.

    - Reflect on three things you are grateful for each morning.

    - Write them down in a gratitude journal to reinforce the positive emotions associated with gratitude.

2. **Mindful Awakening:** Instead of rushing out of bed, take a few moments to awaken your body and mind mindfully. Stretch gently, take deep breaths, and set an intention for the day ahead. This mindful awakening prepares you mentally and physically for the tasks and challenges that lie ahead.

3. **Positive Affirmations**: Incorporate positive affirmations into your morning routine to boost your confidence and mindset. Repeat affirmations that resonate with you, such as "I am capable of overcoming any challenge" or "Today, I choose joy and positivity."

4. **Healthy Breakfast**: Fuel your body with a nutritious breakfast. Eating well-balanced meals supports your physical and mental well-being, providing you with the energy you need to stay focused and positive throughout the day.

Setting a Positive Tone for the Day

1. **Avoid Information Overload**: Limit exposure to negative news and social media first thing in the morning. Instead, start your day with uplifting content or inspirational readings that motivate and inspire you.

2. **Plan Your Day:** Take a few minutes to plan your tasks and priorities for the day ahead. Setting clear goals and priorities helps you stay organized and reduces stress, allowing you to approach your day with a positive and proactive mindset.

3. **Connect with Loved Ones**: If possible, spend quality time with loved ones in the morning. Positive social interactions boost your mood and provide emotional support, setting a positive tone for the rest of your day.

Case Study: The Power of Morning Rituals

Consider the example of successful entrepreneurs who credit their morning rituals for their productivity and success. Tim Cook, CEO of Apple, starts his day early with a morning workout and quiet time for reflection. This routine helps him clear his mind, prioritize his tasks, and approach each day with a positive and focused mindset. By incorporating intentional morning rituals, you too can enhance your productivity and well-being.

2. Mindfulness and Meditation

Mindfulness and meditation are powerful practices that promote mental clarity, emotional resilience, and a present-focused mindset. In our increasingly busy lives, cultivating mindfulness helps us stay grounded in the present moment, appreciating life's experiences with greater awareness and positivity.

Incorporating Mindfulness Practices into Daily Life

1. **Mindful Breathing**: Take a few moments throughout your day to focus on your breath. Deep breathing calms the mind, reduces stress, and enhances your ability to respond to challenges with clarity and composure.

- Practice deep breathing exercises for a few minutes each morning or whenever you feel stressed.

- Focus on the sensation of your breath as it enters and leaves your body, anchoring yourself in the present moment.

2. **Mindful Eating**: Pay attention to your eating habits and savor each bite mindfully. Eating mindfully enhances your enjoyment of food, improves digestion, and promotes healthier eating habits.

- Slow down and chew your food thoroughly.
- Notice the flavors, textures, and sensations of each bite.

3. **Mindful Walking:** Take a mindful walk outdoors to reconnect with nature and clear your mind. Notice the sights, sounds, and sensations around you without judgment, allowing yourself to fully experience the present moment.

- Focus on each step you take and the feeling of your feet touching the ground.
- Appreciate the beauty of your surroundings, whether you're walking in a park, along a beach, or through your neighborhood.

Cultivating a Present and Positive Mindset

1. **Letting Go of Judgment:** Practice non-judgmental awareness of your thoughts and emotions. Instead of reacting impulsively, observe your thoughts with curiosity and compassion. This mindfulness practice reduces stress and fosters a positive outlook on life.

2. **Gratitude Meditation**: Incorporate gratitude into your meditation practice by focusing on what you are grateful for. Gratitude meditation cultivates a sense of appreciation and contentment, strengthening your resilience and well-being.

- o Sit quietly and bring to mind three things you are grateful for.
- o Reflect on why you are grateful for each experience or person in your life.

3. **Body Scan Meditation**: Perform a body scan meditation to promote relaxation and awareness of bodily sensations. This practice helps you release tension, improve self-awareness, and cultivate a positive relationship with your body.

- o Start from your toes and gradually move your attention up to your head.
- o Notice any areas of tension or discomfort and breathe into them with acceptance and kindness.

In conclusion, cultivating daily habits for positivity, such as morning rituals, mindfulness, and meditation, empowers you to approach each day with intention, resilience, and gratitude. These practices not only enhance your mental and emotional well-being but also contribute to your overall satisfaction and success in life.

As you integrate these habits into your daily routine, remember that consistency is key. Start small, stay committed, and observe how these practices transform your mindset and elevate your life. May your journey towards positivity be filled with moments of peace, growth, and profound self-discovery.

Thank you for accompanying me on this transformative exploration. Together, let us continue to embrace the power of daily habits for positivity and create a brighter future, one mindful moment at a time.

Conclusion

Embracing the Power of Positive Thinking

"Your life does not get better by chance; it gets better by change."

- Jim Rohn

As we conclude our journey through the transformative landscape of positive thinking, it's essential to reflect on the profound impact of cultivating a positive mindset and integrating it into our daily lives. Throughout this exploration, we've uncovered invaluable insights and practical strategies that empower us to navigate challenges with resilience, foster meaningful connections, and achieve our aspirations with unwavering determination.

Recap of Key Concepts and Strategies

Throughout this book, we have explored the multifaceted dimensions of positive thinking and its implications for personal growth and success. Let's recap some of the key concepts and strategies that have emerged:

1. **Understanding Positive Thinking**: Positive thinking is not merely about seeing the world through rose-colored glasses. It's a mindset characterized by optimism, resilience, and proactive problem-solving. By adopting a positive outlook, we reframe challenges as opportunities for growth and cultivate an empowering belief in our ability to shape our destiny.

2. **Psychological and Physical Benefits**: Embracing positive thinking has been linked to numerous benefits for our mental and physical well-being. From reducing stress and enhancing emotional resilience to boosting immune function and overall health, the effects of positivity ripple through every aspect of our lives, promoting longevity and vitality.

3. **Strategies for Cultivating Positivity**: We've delved into practical strategies that empower us to cultivate positivity daily:

- **Gratitude Practices**: By keeping a gratitude journal and recognizing the abundance in our lives, we cultivate a mindset of appreciation and contentment.

- **Mindfulness and Meditation**: Incorporating mindfulness practices helps us stay grounded in the present moment, fostering clarity of thought and emotional balance.

- **Positive Affirmations and Visualization**: Harnessing the power of affirmations and visualization techniques strengthens our belief in our goals and enhances our motivation to pursue them relentlessly.

- **Resilience and Positive Communication**: Developing resilience equips us to bounce back from setbacks, while positive communication fosters harmonious relationships and collaborative environments.

- **Goal Setting with Positivity**: Aligning our goals with a positive mindset provides us with direction and purpose, fueling our determination to achieve extraordinary outcomes.

4. Creating a Positive Work Environment: We explored how fostering positivity in the workplace enhances productivity, innovation, and employee satisfaction. By promoting open communication, recognizing achievements, and supporting personal growth, organizations can cultivate a culture where positivity thrives.

Reinforcing the Transformative Impact of a Positive Mindset

The transformative impact of a positive mindset extends far beyond individual well-being; it shapes our interactions with others and influences the communities we inhabit. By embracing positivity, we not only elevate our own lives but also inspire those around us to adopt a similar outlook. Our optimism becomes a beacon of hope, resilience, and possibility in a world often challenged by uncertainty and adversity.

Positive thinking isn't just a fleeting sentiment—it's a powerful force that empowers us to create meaningful change and contribute positively to the world. It enables us to see setbacks as stepping stones to success, failures as opportunities for learning, and challenges as catalysts for growth. With each deliberate choice to approach life with optimism, we reaffirm our capacity to shape a brighter future for ourselves and those we touch.

Encouraging a Lifelong Positive Thinking Journey

As we conclude this exploration, I encourage you, dear reader, to embark on a lifelong journey of positive thinking. Let positivity become not just a habit but a way of life—a guiding principle that enriches your experiences, deepens your relationships, and propels you towards fulfilment.

1. Embracing Ongoing Practice: Positive thinking is a continuous practice that requires dedication and intentionality. Just as we nurture our physical health through exercise and nutrition, so too must we cultivate our mental and emotional well-being through positive thinking habits. Start each day with gratitude, engage in mindfulness exercises, and reinforce your beliefs with affirmations that affirm your potential and worth.

2. Inspiring Others: Your commitment to positivity has the power to inspire others to adopt a similar mindset. Lead by example in your personal and professional interactions, embodying compassion, resilience, and optimism. By sharing your journey and uplifting those around you, you contribute to a collective ripple effect of positivity that transcends boundaries and transforms lives.

3. Perseverance in Adversity: Remember that positivity is not the absence of challenges but the courage to confront them with grace and fortitude. During difficult times, draw strength from within, lean on your support network, and reframe setbacks as opportunities for growth. Your resilience in adversity becomes a testament to the transformative power of positive thinking.

In conclusion, the journey of embracing the power of positive thinking is both empowering and enlightening. It invites us to cultivate a mindset that embraces possibilities, nurtures resilience, and fosters genuine happiness. As you continue to integrate these principles into your life, may you discover an abundance of joy, fulfilment, and purpose.

Thank you for accompanying me on this enriching exploration. Together, let us continue to illuminate the world with positivity, one thought and action at a time. Here's to a future filled with boundless optimism and endless opportunities for growth and prosperity.

REFERENCES

1. **Fredrickson, B. L., & Joiner, T. (2002). Positive emotions trigger upward spirals toward emotional well-being. Psychological Science, 13(2), 172-175

2. Beck, A. T. (1976). Cognitive Therapy and the Emotional Disorders. International Universities Press.

3. Seligman, M. E. P. (1991). Learned Optimism: How to Change Your Mind and Your Life. Pocket Books.

4. Dweck, C. S. (2006). Mindset: The New Psychology of Success. Random House.

5. Emmons, R. A., & McCullough, M. E. (2003). Counting Blessings Versus Burdens: An Experimental Investigation of Gratitude and Subjective Well-Being in Daily Life. Journal of Personality and Social Psychology, 84(2), 377–389.

6. Burns, D. D. (1980). Feeling Good: The New Mood Therapy. HarperCollins.

7. Gollwitzer, P. M., & Oettingen, G. (2011). Planning Promotes Goal Striving. In K. D. Vohs & R. F. Baumeister (Eds.), Handbook of Self-Regulation:

Research, Theory, and Applications (pp. 162-185). Guilford Press.

8. Carver, C. S., & Scheier, M. F. (2002). Optimism and Pessimism. In C. R. Snyder & S. J. Lopez (Eds.), Handbook of Positive Psychology (pp. 231-243). Oxford University Press.

9. Reivich, K., & Shatté, A. (2002). The Resilience Factor: 7 Keys to Finding Your Inner Strength and Overcoming Life's Hurdles. Broadway Books.

10. Fredrickson, B. L. (2001). The Role of Positive Emotions in Positive Psychology: The Broaden-and-Build Theory of Positive Emotions. American Psychologist, 56(3), 218-226.

11. Goleman, D. (1998). Working with Emotional Intelligence. Bantam Books.

12. Fredrickson, B. L. (2009). Positivity: Top-Notch Research Reveals the Upward Spiral That Will Change Your Life. Crown Publishing Group.

13. Kabat-Zinn, J. (1990). Full Catastrophe Living: Using the Wisdom of Your Body and Mind to Face Stress, Pain, and Illness. Delta.

14. Harris, D. (2014). 10% Happier: How I Tamed the Voice in My Head, Reduced Stress Without Losing My Edge,

and Found Self-Help That Actually Works – A True Story. Dey Street Books.

15. Salzberg, S. (1995). Lovingkindness: The Revolutionary Art of Happiness. Shambhala Publications.

16. Siegel, D. J. (2010). The Mindful Brain: Reflection and Attunement in the Cultivation of Well-Being. W. W. Norton & Company.

ABOUT THE AUTHOR

Mahuya Gupta (B.Sc, B.Tech, M.Sc Engg, MBA), the author of *"Secrets to Leverage The Power of Focus,"* is a dynamic professional whose career has traversed diverse realms. With a background in Applied Physics and Engineering, she honed her skills in the corporate arena, progressing from an entry-level position to a senior management role within a renowned multinational corporation in India.

A passion for writing kindled in her school days has always burned brightly within her, earning the admiration of her teachers. Although this creative pursuit took a backseat during her higher education and corporate journey, it is now rekindled with vigor through this book.

Mahuya's writing is informed by extensive research and a wealth of knowledge accumulated over her 20+ years in the corporate world. Beyond her literary endeavors, Mahuya is a multi-talented artist, proficient in various mediums of painting and a skilled violinist, with a trove of accolades garnered during her academic journey.

Other books written by Mahuya:

1. Series - The Secrets to Success:

   - Secrets To Leverage The Power of Focus
   - Secrets to Turn Failure into Success
   - Secrets to Build Unstoppable Success Habits

2. Series - Radiant Mindset

   - Harnessing the Power of Positivity
   - How to Embrace Positive Transformation

She can be contacted at authormahuya@gmail.com, inviting readers to engage in meaningful conversations about focus, creativity, and her diverse passions.

Disclaimer

The information provided in this book is for educational and informational purposes only and is not intended as a substitute for professional advice. While every effort has been made to ensure the accuracy and completeness of the information contained herein, the author and publisher assume no responsibility for errors, inaccuracies, omissions, or any outcomes related to the use of this information.

The strategies and techniques discussed are based on the author's personal experiences and research and may not be suitable for everyone. Readers should consult with a qualified professional before applying any of the advice or strategies mentioned in this book.

By reading this book, you acknowledge and agree to these terms.

May I Ask You For A Small Favor?

First, I want to thank you for taking the time to read this book. You could have chosen any other book, but you took mine, and I totally appreciate this.

I hope you got at least a few actionable insights that will have a positive impact on your day-to-day life.

Can I ask for 30 seconds more of your time?

I'd love it if you could leave a review about the book. Reviews may not matter to big-name authors, but they're a tremendous help for authors like me, who don't have much following. They help me to grow my readership by encouraging folks to take a chance on my books.

To put it straight - reviews are the lifeblood of any author. Kindly visit the store where you bought this book to provide your valuable review.

It will just take less than a minute of your time, but it will tremendously help me to reach out to more people, so please leave your review. Thanks for your support of my work. And I'd love to see your review.

Other Books Written By The Author

Click here to buy

Click here to buy

Click here to buy

Click here to buy

Click here to buy

www.ingramcontent.com/pod-product-compliance
Lightning Source LLC
Chambersburg PA
CBHW070154230526
45471CB00002B/666